Karl Heinzen

What is real democracy?

Answered by an exposition of the Constitution of the United States

Karl Heinzen

What is real democracy?
Answered by an exposition of the Constitution of the United States

ISBN/EAN: 9783337733315

Printed in Europe, USA, Canada, Australia, Japan

Cover: Foto ©ninafisch / pixelio.de

More available books at **www.hansebooks.com**

WHAT IS REAL DEMOCRACY?

ANSWERED BY AN EXPOSITION OF THE CONSTITUTION OF THE UNITED STATES.

BY KARL HEINZEN.

Published as a Precursor to the Presidential Campaign,

BY THE

ASSOCIATION FOR THE PROPAGATION OF RADICAL PRINCIPLES.

H. LIEBER, INDIANAPOLIS, INDIANA.

1871.

WHAT IS REAL DEMOCRACY?

AGENCIES OF DEVELOPMENT IN THE STATE.

A term only belonging, in fact, to the realm of natural
history, and the world of elements, has become current among
historians and politicians, although by them analogously
applied,—we mean the expression 'organic development.'
It is most often made use of by those teachers of statesmanship who have need of some palliating or imposing phrase by
which to defend or support that which exists, particularly
that·among existing things 'which deserves to be destroyed.'
But even liberal politicians still seriously engage in discussion
of the question whether States, like plants, develop 'organ-
ically', that is to say, by means of an unconscious, limited
growth, determined by the first germ, or whether, in their
origin and development, they are and should be the mutable
work of the thinking and directing mind of man : in other
words, the question would be—Is man an unconscious production of nature, like the plant? or is he a self-conscious,
self-determining, thinking being? If he is the latter, no one
who agrees to this will care to take upon himself the respon-
sibility of the doctrine that an *association* of those self-
conscious, self-determining, thinking beings, in regulating
their affairs, are obliged to give up or do away with that
which is the greatest advantage of the single individual ;
that if common sense and his own interests bid the single

individual undo a step in the wrong direction, turn back upon a false path, rectify a committed mistake, an organized union of single individuals might follow common sense and preserve their interest by doing just the reverse of all this : and yet the teachings of the organic development of States is nothing but this nonsensical doctrine in an other garb. It is a coarse mysticism, yet involved in the superstitions of former times, which, however, suits equally well both that indolent thoughtlessness which does not take the trouble to arrive at any clearness in regard to the questions naturally arising in an organized society, and that pseudo-democratic prudence which fancies that all political problems may be solved by a shiftless *laissey aller*, as well as that reactionary spirit of calculation which attempts to keep the influence of thinking minds at a distance from political development, so that every 'historical' wrong may grow on unchecked. Again, this mysticism is closely allied to that pernicious, bigoted belief that ascribes all evil issues and events brought about by the folly of men, as well as every fortunate turn their heedlessness has not deserved, to some superhuman power or dispensation, so that one does not tend to increase their prudence, nor the other to stimulate their energies. Have they caused a misfortune, by some action or non-action, then they save themselves from a recognition of their guilt by pointing to the will of providence. Have they escaped some danger, with 'more luck than sense,' to which their carelessness had exposed them, then they avoid reflecting upon the conditions of their future safety by rendering thanks to a merciful Supreme Being.

If ten intelligent men, having a common purpose, should constitute themselves a society, it would not enter their minds to rely, for attaining their object, upon 'organic development', which they can not survey, nor yet hold in their own hands ; but after examining, and agreeing upon the conditions of their union, they will expect success only from a correct choice of the needful ways and means,—in short, from their own intelligence and activity. Should they come to the conclusion that they have made a mistake, or started from a false principle, they will correct their own work. It is exactly the same with an intelligent State, except that here the interests are multiplied, and the greater number of members, as well as the extension of space, make a rapid survey and communication difficult and complicated. But this complication, instead of justifying a thought- and action-less falling back upon the mysticism of 'organic development', makes rather the imperative demand upon us to so act upon the universal understanding that the nature and aim of society will become clear to all, and to simplify the mechanism of the State as much as possible.

Of course, the more primitively a State is constituted the more forcibly will its condition and development recall organic, natural formations; but a purely organic, political development, effected only by a blind pressure forward, or a state of unconscious, uncontrollable growth, existing in present elements and circumstances, was never known. Every State, even the most uncivilized of the remotest past, was an artificial production which, at least in its chief, claimed for itself all the intellectual powers existing at the time. So many of its elements as excluded themselves from taking an intelligent part in public proceedings were but material made use of by the other elements: its further development, however, only consisted, and could only consist, in the increase of those elements who took such active, intelligent part. If we picture to ourselves a political association numbering thirty or fifty millions of clear-minded, intelligent people who all recognize and claim their just part in the community on the basis of perfect equality, we shall find that not an inch of room is left for a mysterious 'organic development'; and all manifestations, all actions, all reforms, every step of progress made in the State, will be the pre-calculated result of the intelligent action of these thirty or fifty millions.

While we thus banish all mystical views that would make political activity and development dependent upon mysterious laws or powers that may not be controlled by the members of the State, we are far from losing sight of the outer conditions of development, from considering the necessary effects of natural causes as disposed of, and of excluding from our calculations the obstacles brought about by given circumstances, for, in short, from imagining that we may govern by the speculative mind alone, every element and actual fact that exerts an influence on society, or perhaps even do away with, by ignoring, it. To make our calculations according to existing circumstances is a requirement that we need not particularly recall to even the most ordinary mind. What we must recall, however, is the requirement that circumstances must be acted upon with *intelligence*. Wherever these two contradict each other, we must simply put the question whether circumstances or intelligence shall give way. Whoever decides against the latter has ' organic development' with him, and must suffer the consequences. Kingship, aristocracy, slavery, are historical institutions whose advocates attempt to perpetuate as the basis of 'organic development'. Whosoever does not oppose this pretension with the peremptory demand made by reason, that those institutions must be completely abolished, will wait in vain to see the republic, equality, liberty, developed from their 'evolution'. A sensible politician will just as little expect freedom when the conditions that naturally lead to it do nöt exist as demand equal performances of unequal abilities, or hope to make new circumstances without the necessary preparations. Ask the present Chinese, for instance, to proclaim a republic, of which they have so far not the slightest idea or conception. The question is to follow up recognized and indisputable aims, in the direction of which development according to *reason*, not according to given circumstances, goes on, in spite of all obstacles and under all conditions ; not to sacrifice the general principles of reason to any regard for particular circumstances, or because of the difficulty of their immediate execution ; and not to expect progress of any mysterious agencies, but to call to mind upon every occasion this truth — The attainment of any progressive aims solely depends, and must depend, on the intelligence and will of the members of the State. Is it impossible for the Chinese to be republicans just yet, then must the republicans not turn Chinese on their account, but wait until the sons of the Celestial Empire may some time establish a republic too, and labor to that effect. Of the spirit of serfdom they will be cured by no organic development, but only by the gradual rise and progress of republican views and convictions, whether these be brought into active play by the extreme consequences of present circumstances or by a train of abstract reasoning.

Where some perceive ' organic development' others would see the 'logic of events', which is wont to accompany the former. Both terms point to similar conditions, that is, such in which human beings are surprised and pushed forward by effects whose causes they either created or suffered to exist, through obstinacy or want of foresight. That there is logic in events is as much as to say, in these cases, that those who brought them about had none. He who holds fast to the logic of correct principles is saved from the logic of events, which, to give it an other name, is nothing but the ill experience caused by unlogical action. It is only possible to foresee consequences through the recognition of principles whose embodiment or realization constitutes actual development. History shows that nations as well as their rulers were scourged and punished and compelled to change their action by the logic of events, because they did not permit themselves to be taught, guided, and warned by the logic of principles. Wherever they progressed, they did so because they were obliged to, not because such was their intention : they abandoned the old because it had grown to be untenable and insupportable, not because they had in advance recognized or aimed at the new. Even slavery was not abolished in the Republic of North America because the nation had recognized its wrong in principle, and calculated its destructive consequences in advance, but because these unlooked-for consequences swelled into a fearful evil that threatened to overwhelm the country. The logic of events forced the people at last to acknowledge their want of logic in principle by at least annihilating its consequences. As professor of the logic of events, Jefferson Davis had to teach them what they had not learned of the former Jefferson, the teacher of the logic of justice. This lesson however, paid for at so dear a cost, which recent events have taught them, will be entirely lost upon them in other questions if they have not through it arrived at the conclusion that principles altogether must constitute the line of conduct in the development of the State, of the *whole* State, and that the 'organic development' of conditions and institutions that exist in contradiction to correct principles is nothing but a growth of destruction.

The great question arises whether the nations, after reaping for thousands of years only misfortune and misery from the 'organic development' of existing circumstances and perverse institutions, and after having been shown the consequences of their want of foresight and timely resolution by the logic of events, will not arrive at length at such a standpoint of intelligence and energy as will enable them to so form their own destinies with clear self-determination, according to the immutable laws of right and reason, so organize their relations to each other, so secure their reforms, and thereby balance their interests, that they may in future be spared from oppression as well as plunder, wars as well as revolutions, in short, from all former calamities and convulsions. Not organic development but developed organization is the means to this end. As in physics, thus in politics prevention should make the cure unnecessary. Of course, it is only possible for the people to possess the capacities for this under a democratic form of government, where free expression, according to generally accepted rules, is secured to all desires and interests ; and since we are to analyze the question what constitutes true democracy, our first task was to purify the ground on which it is to be built up, from all the obscuring fogs of mystical views and beliefs. A people possessing a democratic organization may attain every thing it requires ; and for every thing it lacks, a people possessing a democratic organization is itself responsible.

---o---

CHIEF CONDITIONS OF TRUE DEMOCRACY.

Perhaps the word 'democracy' suffers even more abuse than the word 'freedom'. What were the southern slaveholders fighting for in the war of the rebellion? Every third word with them was their 'liberty',—that was to say, the liberty to make slaves of other human beings. Every European despot does battle for the 'liberty of his people' when he leads them on to be slaughtered in his struggle with some foreign despot, his competitor in the business of oppression. L. Napoleon, a chief representative of this liberty, was at the same time democratic through and through. Sword in hand, he drove the people to the polls, so as to put an end to all democracy by his 'democratic' election to the imperial throne. In a similar manner, he attempted to make Mexico happy by one of his colleagues, who he said was 'democratically chosen.' In Prussia, whose king, as emperor of Germany, also discovered Napoleonic 'liberty', all are with characteristic modesty called 'democratic' who do not actually swear by the absolute rulership of 'by the grace of God'. The English, with their inviolable queen, whose whole task seems to consist in furnishing as large a number of descendants as possible, on which the property of her subjects may be squandered, with their privileged aristocracy, that owns almost all the soil in the country, and their six millions of paupers who have no right to vote, consider themselves the first democrats in the world. They are only excelled by the 'democrats' of this country, who discovered the spirit of true democracy to consist in the unchecked trade in human flesh, and in the right of parts of the State to commit with impunity crimes against the whole of the State, in the name of Slavery.

In view of such a misuse of language, and such a falsification of conception, it is necessary in a few words to explain true democracy, and define its conditions.

By the people, unless it permits itself to be degraded by some despot to an irresponsible herd of subjects, we understand not some select or separate part of the body politic, but the *whole* population dwelling upon the soil of the State. The people and the nation in this sense are one. The government of the people (democracy) then means the government of the *whole* population, or nation (so far as it is not excluded from participation in it for particularly valid causes, such as minority or loss of reason). Democracy without an equality of rights of the *whole people* is a contradiction in terms. The authorization of one part of the population to govern, with the exclusion of any one other, is even in its mildest form aristocracy, or ochlocracy, but not democracy. And if a so-called demo-cratic body politic of one hundred millions exclude only the smallest fraction of its number, say one hundred individuals, from the right to vote, it will consist of one hundred millions less one hundred *aristocrats*. So long however as the equal rights of *women* are not acknowledged, true, complete democracy is out of the question anywhere: so far only andro-cracy exists all over the world.

So soon as the participation of the *whole* people is necessary for the realization of democracy, it also requires a common center, where the universal will may manifest itself, and be put into action. A scattering of this manifestation and putting into action necessarily destroys the unity of the people, and changes democracy into anarchy. A sovereignty of States or provinces or communites would be the absolute dissolution of the State.

Democratic principles are always put into practice through the votes of the majority. This majority, however, can only be justified in its action if, and so long as, it grants to the minority the same means of action and of expression as are possessed and made use of by itself. Without unlimited freedom of the press, and of public discussion for all, and of everything, it is as impossible to think of democracy as without equal rights before the law and at the polls.

No citizen is bound to recognize a government in whose establishment he was not able to cooperate by freely giving his vote : none is bound to obey laws that were made without his consent. Such a government would be a despotism to him, and such laws only dictates of absolute power.

Democracy is destroyed so soon as it institutes a power which is capable of opposing the will of the people, or of leaving it unexecuted. The will of the people is, and must be, the sole law ; and to execute this law, tools, but not rulers, are needed. In order to be really able to rule, the will of the people should be manifested as directly as possible both in making and in executing the laws. Their will must not be suspended in order to delegate its power to officials, or its sovereignty to representatives. As it is always in their pleasure to undo again acts they have concluded, so must they always be able to dispose of the agents entrusted with the execution of those acts. These agents must not only be accountable to but also ever dependent on the people. As there should not exist in the State any institutions or any law, any power or any court, which is not an expression or a tool of the will of the people, so should there be none either that might hamper it or exclude themselves from its jurisdiction.

These, then, are in brief the chief conditions òf a real or direct democracy, without which there can be no true freedom, no lasting security, no universal progress. In the course of our examination, we shall see in how far the constitution of the United States, that has heretofore always been regarded as an ideal of democratic institutions, fulfils these conditions.

---o---

COMPROMISE AND PRINCIPLE.

We have just made the demand that not the unchecked natural growth of that which exists, or that which has accidentally originated,—this being called organic development, —but the leading principle of reason should shape and guide the movements of the body politic. Of course we do not by this make the assertion that this leading principle existed, and could exist, from the beginning. It is not necessary to teach anyone any more that States did not at first spring into being as the embodyment of pre-developed theories, but through the cooperation and putting to use of existing, actual circumstances, often enough brought about by mere accident. Theories, only developed from experiences supplied by this cooperation of circumstances, and reforms at first were nothing but the result of unforeseen evils. In this manner, however, some insight was gradually gained, and the attempt made to subordinate given circumstances to the theories that had been developed from experience, and to remodel the body politic according to these. Sparta made such an experiment through Lycurgus, Athens through Solon; and every people that after a revolution adopted a new constitution did the same. The success of such remodeling, however, always depends on two conditions,—first, in the establishment of correct principles for the future, and, secondly, in the annihilation of the destructive elements of the past. Yet, it is exactly the neglect of these conditions which generally defeats these attempts at reformation. Even when correct principles for the future have been found, either insight or determination or power is wanting to sufficiently do away with the destructive remnants of the circumstances that have been triumphed over for the present. They are generally again assimilated with the process of development, either by silent connivance or by a compromise, where confidence in the effect of the victory won, and the progress of time, serves as the deceptive mediator; and the consequence is wont to be that these elements, by the aid of old connections, means, and experiences, gradually regain their former power, and then again necessitate a new and still more thorough reformation. Every compromise, then, that does not *at least completely secure* the gradual supplanting of the old by the new is nothing but the apparent cancelation of an old debt by the contraction of a new, or the eradication of one disease by the inoculation of an other.

The danger attending the conclusion of a compromise is all the greater the more we are deceived in its nature. Whoever adopts something that, at certain times and under certain circumstances, may have served as an expedient to escape certain embarrassments as a cure on this account, at all times and under all circumstances, and as a preventive of all embarrassments, condemns himself to an everlasting struggle with evils that he considers benefits; and, by mistaking their nature, cuts off all means of having them removed.

Whoever may desire to have a striking proof of the truth

of these remarks, let him look back on the struggles that have grown out of the constitution of the United States, while the people were continually praising this same constitution as the panacea of all evils, and desired to preserve it unchanged.

The constitution of the United States is the result of a four-fold compromise : —

Firstly, of unity with individual interests,—of national sovereignty with the so-called sovereignty of States.

Secondly, of the republic with monarchy.

Thirdly, of freedom with slavery.

Fourthly, of democracy with aristocracy.

It is founded, therefore, on the four-fold combination of *principles perfectly incompatible, and eternally excluding each other*,— founded for the purpose of equally preserving these principles in spite of their incompatibility, and of carrying out their practical results,—in other words, for the purpose of making an impossible thing possible.

This combination, and the contradiction of principles which it covers, was only partially recognized when the constitution was first drawn up ; and most people do not recognize it yet. The constitution had momentarily served the purpose of uniting under difficult circumstances contradictory elements to one apparently harmonious whole ; moreover, it certainly possessed indisputable advantages that favorably distinguished it from other constitutions ; and this was sufficient for its admirers to set it up as an unsurpassable, inviolable model for all times. Even all these advantages for development, which the United States owed only to the natural qualifications and the isolated position of their country, were ascribed to the influence of a constitution which in some other country, more exposed to the influence of heterogenious surroundings, might not have remained unchanged ten years. But these deceptions not only did not check the antagonism of incompatible elements, secured by the constitution, and apparent in all the history of the United States, but they made it even more destructive since its causes were not clearly perceived, and, therefore, the means to end it not adopted.

Only in regard to *one* contradiction clearness has been gained. The rebellion of the slaveholders has opened the eyes of even the most devoted admirers of the constitution to the fact that freedom and slavery can not exist together, even in the name of the great founders of the republic and that of the much-praised union. A distinguished American statesman strikingly characterized this constitutional copulation by the remark that "the war of the rebellion was waged in order to expound the constitution." A most costly constitution which requires such expounding! Those who but a short time back desired to preserve this cherished constitution unchanged at every price now congratulate themselves that an amendment has delivered them from the unpleasant task of serving both as an authority for as well as a protection to two principles eternally at war with each other to the death. Since a beginning has been made, however, with this one amendment, and its most necessary supplements, propositions for a dozen other amendments have already followed in its train,—all called forth by that one evil, slavery, now abolished at least in name and principle.

Should not this be an inducement to even the most contented admirers of things as they are to reflect on the other hostile principles as contradictions which men still attempt to keep united by the paragraphs and the authority of the constitution, whose union, however, must and will prove in its practical consequences as impossible to preserve, and in part as pernicious, as that of freedom with slavery? Are we to wait till here, too, we are taught better by experiences that must be paid for by incalculable sacrifices? Is the constitution to retain its other defects, too, till it is 'expounded' by civil war? or shall we conclude to listen to reason while it is yet time? permit the critical analysis of an age that has since made a great step forward to take the place of the blind worship of institutions of former times, and learn to trust in immutable principles more than in untenable compromises?

It seems to us the time is not far distant when the people of the United States should prepare for a national convention, there to remodel their constitution in the spirit of true democracy. A short critical review may help to point the way.

---o---

ORIGIN OF THE UNION.

In general, compromises have been the practical means of reformation and transition in political developments. Of the United States, however, it might be said that they came into the world with a compromise. and through a compromise. Their original members were still less prepared for a union than for a republic. The different English colonies, having sprung into being through associations for settlements, and grants of land to single founders, had so little in common that they were not even permitted to carry on trade with each other. Outer circumstances first forced them to unite,—the same power, moreover, which had separated them. Only the arbitrary act of taxation without representation, that pressed equally on all, the Stamp Act, the duty on imports, and similar annoyances, roused a spirit of unity and a desire for association. But even upon this desire no action was taken till it rose into a positive. exacting necessity ; so that in the beginning only seven of the colonies came to the joint conclusion of declaring themselves independent ; the other six entered the union at a later period ; and only the war against England induced them in 1776 to establish a confederacy.

But even in this confederacy there was so little true patriotism and public spirit to be found that without a French loan and the aid of Generals Rochambeau and Lafayette, who made it possible for Washington to win the decisive victories of New York and Yorktown, the whole movement would probably have failed. It is questionable, too, whether without France, which in 1783 concluded the peace of Versailles with England, and therein stipulated the independence of North America, that independence would have been preserved and maintained.

After the conclusion of peace, however, the evils of a loose connection, brought about only by outward dangers, became more than ever apparent. There was only the choice between a closer union or new isolation of the single States ; universal dismemberment was to be prevented ; and after the confederation had barely escaped the danger of being broken up again by the struggles of the federalists and democrats, it was not till 1787 that the constitution was adopted, and the union firmly established, all conflicting party interests and embarrassments of the varying parts of the country being spared and protected as much as possible by compromises. Let us consider first

———o———

THE COMPROMISE BETWEEN A UNITED STATE AND A CONFEDERACY.

What, then, was this union and confederacy? *An absolutely necessary association* of different colonies that originally had nothing in common but their oppressor, and were brought together by nothing but the common war against him. Neither

a natural impulse nor an originally common interest was the
tie of their union, and their party egotism insisted on making
this tie as loose as possible, for which reason they did not rise
to the conception of one common *State*, but attempted to perpetuate their individual existence as united *States*. And this
accidental association of political individuals, founded through
no inner necessity, but brought about by outward considerations, and even yet marked as single corporations by a constitutional stamp of separation,— this association is to be looked
upon as the most perfect embodyment of the conception of an
ideal State! making a virtue of necessity, that is to be set
up for a model of creation, which in fact was nothing but a
work of expediency at a time of temporary danger from without, and then was barely changed into an expedient to serve
interior purposes also. We should be very desirous to hear
the answer of some genuine defender of the federal system
to the question what the fathers of this republic would have
done, or should have done, if only a single colony had existed
at the time of the declaration of independence in place of
thirteen. Would they have divided or dismembered this
one and made thirteen of it in order to form ‘United States’
instead of a united State, and thus realize the present so
highly-lauded ideal, where the single members, with their
individual egotism, still constantly rebel against the common
interests of the whole body? They would have been content
with that division which the *mechanism of government* requires
in every larger State, that is, with the classification into
counties, districts, and communities, and the proposition to
introduce a spirit of *dualism* into their union, by the formation
of States to be as independent as possible, would certainly
have appeared to them like intentional treason. The predilection of Americans for the character of their confederacy,
which has given them so much trouble already, and even
through its adopted child, slavery, brought them to the brink
of ruin, can only be explained by the blind prejudice that

long habit is wont to produce, and that occasionally amounts to actual ridiculousness. Nowhere, however, has this predilection appeared more ridiculous than in President Grant's message of February 7th of this year, where he recommends congress to elevate the character of the embassy to the German 'Empire', but just newly cemented with blood, by an increase of salary. In this message he makes the discovery that the military connection of the German States, under a caricature of the bug-bear in Kyffhäuser, "in some manner resembles the American Union", and must, therefore, "arouse the deep sympathy of the people of the United States." He sees in this "event" an adoption of "the American system of union", while it does not disturb him in the least to be obliged to acknowledge that the separate German 'fatherlands' were divided and separated by the dynastical jealousy and the ambition of short-sighted rulers. But the German fatherlands were not only separated by, they also *originated* through, these rulers, formerly plundering knights-errant, who stole a piece of land with their two-legged chattels, and later, according to how much more they stole, or bought, or inherited, assumed the title of duke, king, etc. Now, instead of starting from the idea that these thieves, who stole land and human beings, should not have existed at all, or been swept from off the face of the earth as soon as possible, by which the division and separation of the German people would have been prevented at the very outset, our statesman, General Grant, considers the existence of these thieves, and the separation caused by them, as a necessary and desirable condition, so that at a later period might spring from it the possibility and necessity of a union, and perceives in this the development of his American ideal State. It is almost like breaking a man's arms and legs, in order to make his limbs barely whole again by a superficial cure, and then setting him up as a model of good health to those who have always enjoyed unbroken limbs; and if this model, then, meets a companion who has undergone the same fate, suffered the same misfortune, he feels "deep sympathy" with him, and proudly congratulates him on the advantage of having mended limbs like himself, instead of sound ones like foolish, common-place people.

So long as this planet is in existence, no united State ever yet sprung into being of its own accord from natural impulse as the manifestation of an inner necessity, or the embodyment of an original conception of a State. All united States were established through outward causes. They were always the children of the distress caused by outside wars ; and when those were over, they became the generators of inner, civil wars. The Greeks were forced into a union by the Persians, the Netherlands by the Spaniards, the Swiss by the Austrians, the North Americans by the English, and the Germans by the French ; and as they all have the same origin, the same fate awaits them all,—either to be separated again by inner dissensions or to be blended into a real, a united, State. This, not taking into any consideration any outward causes, is also an inner, logical necessity : for if the single, united States are strong enough to assert their individuality, they will feel neither the want of subordinating themselves so much to the power of the confederacy that this is enabled to solve its problem, nor any inclination to do so ; and if they are not so strong, they will lose with the power also the purpose for which they might desire to perpetuate their existence as separate States.

To illustrate the necessity of such a course by examples, it is enough to cast a look on the latest history of the most highly-praised confederacies, those of Switzerland and North America. Switzerland attempted to guard the celebrated peculiarities and local difference of interest as much as possible by preserving sovereignty of the cantons. What followed as the consequence? There developed in the sovereign hotbeds of philistinism, of bigotry, of reaction, of treason, such threatening "peculiarities" and contradictions against the common interests of the republic that they endangered the whole confederacy, and the country was obliged to put an end to them by main force through a war; and after this bloody lesson had been taught, the constitution of the confederacy was completely remodeled, so that now the federal government possesses even greater ascendancy over the cantons than the cantons once possessed over the impotent government. Only an other foreign war is needed to force Switzerland to adopt a course that must lead to a united State. And how is it with the North American union, that formerly put forth such tender care for the preservation of Southern peculiarities? A much severer lesson was administered to it by the rebellion of the slaveholders than to the Swiss confederation by the war of the jesuits; but although congress has since then often been obliged to reject and suppress the refractoriness and the individual pretensions of single States in the spirit and in the interest of the common weal, no one appears to have yet arrived at the conclusion that these dissensions can not end before a united State is definitely established, that a federal State is a mistake in principle, and, therefore, in practice, too, and that the local peculiarities to be preserved by it, which are in opposition to the idea of unity, and, therefore, to the common interest, have no right of existence, much less to constitutional protection. The State rights, so jealously guarded by the 'democrats', are in practice but a safe-guard for individual rights; and without them it would have been as impossible for slavery to take root in America as for the rule of the jesuits to grow up in Switzerland. A safe-guard of freedom, however, against the federal power, as their defenders claim for them, they can not logically be for this reason,—that we should then be obliged to assume they would in a given case possess an ascendancy over that power, and thereby annihilate the confederacy. The balance of common and local rights and interests is just as much of an untenable fiction and delusion as that of the balance of the different State powers. In the State, in the democratic State, there can exist but *one* supreme interest, that of the *whole* people, represented in the central government.

It becomes plain from what has been said that the federal State, which is called a safe-guard of democracy, is in truth actually undemocratic, a constant hindrance of true democracy, and a clog on universal progress. In this connection, I need only call to mind the absence of a common code of laws and system of education, to which only now some attention is being given in Washington, and the opposition which all propositions for so-called interior improvements are obliged to contend against there.

The prejudice in favor of the federal State quite commonly entertained may be very simply explained from the fact that it was always only free States, republics, that were wont and able to form a union. In the very nature of the thing, such republics, founded by single communities, are originally small, while monarchies attempt to extend their territory by conquest as soon as possible. When these small republics, then, are threatened by any danger, which generally proceeds from monarchical conquerors, they feel too weak to meet it singly, and the common necessity of defence united them not only for the moment but also makes plain to them what other interests they have in common for whose protection that form of union serves, which is called a federal State. Now, instead of recognizing that those advantages of freedom which federal States are wont to show are to be ascribed only to the original nature of their single individuals, that is, *to the republic in itself*, they are erroneously supposed to be the outgrowth of the *form of their union*, the federal system. Again, monarchies, the representatives of non-freedom, are not capable of real union at all, because they do not admit of any equality of rights among the confederates, but require the predominating action of a single power, towards which the others occupy more or less the position of vassals. Only a Prussian prince who carries on the work of making federal unions by means of 'blood and iron', but was obliged to pause half way, could have had the idea of trying as a momentary expedient an experiment with a monarchical federal State. But whoever enjoys sound eye-sight may already perceive the great black and white sack prepared in which one member of the German confederacy after the other is to disappear, with every one of Grant's "peculiarities"; and if the emperor mania was necessary at any rate, in order to educate the German nation by a pessimistical course up to a republic, it is very desirable that the black and white sack should be filled full as soon as possible. Through a united *monarchy*, the Germans will then be spared from the wearysome labor of attaining a united *republic* by going through a union similar to the American, while France, the much abused, is far in advance in regard to the attainment of such a republic.

---o---

CENTRALIZATION.

This united republic is an actual bug-bear to the adherents of the federal republic. The horrible vision by which they are haunted is the danger of ' *centralization* '. They mean with the evil of the independence of States to contend against the evil of independent centralization, without considering that both evils are unnecessary, and may be equally well abolished at the same time. They would soon forget their fear if they would do away with that want of reflection which builds up the republic on monarchical institutions, and then expects it to show anti-monarchical results. Whoever centralizes the power and the means of the people in a monarchical head, separated from the people, will prove himself a fool if he imagines he may establish a democracy only by giving that head a republican name. Centralized power in the hands of a 'republican' president is only different in name from the centralized power in the hands of a king. If the character of the State, however, be such that the people rule at the pinnacle as well as at the basis, then centralization is the simplest means for the manifestation and execution of the universal will. The center can only rule over the circle, if all power actually proceeds from the former: does the power, however, freely flow into the center from all parts of the circle only to unite there, then this center will be but the form and the means of the universal power that can never become dangerous to itself. It is one of the most preposterous suppositions in the world to believe that a free people, itself holding and exercising its whole power, instead of delivering it up to an independent rule, would ever in the centralization of its will oppose this same will or annul it : could ever turn the government against itself as a means of oppression, after making that government but the means of manifesting and executing its desires : that it would have the same danger to fear from a center which can not exist and work at all without its (the people's) action as from a center to whom it delivers up all action, and all means thereto.

The prejudice against centralization originated through absolute monarchies, particularly through the warning example of France. Here no one takes into consideration, however, that the union of all means of power and of rulership in the hands of an authority outside of and above the people is the direct contrary to a union of those means through the people themselves. If the people surrender their sword to a master, they are in his power ; but, if every citizen has his hand on the hilt of that sword, it is ridiculous to imagine that he will draw it on himself. It is equally ridiculous to fear that the separate parts of the State would make use of their free union in the central government to put fetters on themselves at home, that is, to have the central government rule over the local affairs of the municipalities, as was the case in monarchical, centralizing France. · As a matter of course, they would introduce a constitution for the municipalities, *according to general principles*, like the constitution of ·a State; but they would have no manner of interest in taking its enforcement from the municipal powers, and charging it upon the central government. In France, too, after the monarchical yoke had been thrown off, it became plain that the first desire of the people was the emancipation of the municipal powers from the central government. In short, it is a supposition altogether contradictory in itself that true democracy, which permits of no power outside of the people, should make use of the State as a whole in order to arrange and govern it undemocratically in detail. *The separate executive power*, and the *representative system*, it is these alone which make centralization a danger and a means of oppression, because, as we shall see further on, they entirely exclude real democracy.

---o---

THE COMPROMISE OF MONARCHY WITH THE REPUBLIC.

The question whether there should be a 'united State or a confederation of States' required a detailed answer, because this point is in general so little understood. It touches, too, the chief compromise with which the other compromises of incompatible contradictions are connected, and which gave rise to the constitution of this 'model republic'. The second compromise we have to take into consideration was that of the republic with monarchy. When the constitution of the United States originated there was no proper pattern to copy. The nearest pattern was the constitution of England, under which the United States themselves had grown to power; and against which they would not have rebelled at all had the rights it guarantied been accorded to them as fully as to the mother country. It is not surprising, therefore, that they made the English constitution the basis of their own. It is well known that several of the prominent statesmen of that time were favorably inclined towards a constitutional monarchy, after the model of the English; and equally noted that it only depended on Washington's will to be made king of North America. Had this man, like the brand of European princes, possessed so little self respect as to consider it compatible with his dignity as a man and a human being to permit himself to be degraded to an oppressor of his fellow citizens by having a crown put on his head, this country would now have His Majesty Washington the Xth to worship in place of His Excellency Ulysses the Ist; and the German subject would have no need of perjury any more to remain here too what he was at home. Possibly, the progress made ahead of England might then have consisted only in the introduction of a representative hand-shake on particular occasions, for instance, at the opening of the parliament, that of course would have had its house of lords, or planters, and its house of commons, or business men. But since kingship failed, because of Washington's honorableness, and the radical spirit of a Paine, a Jefferson, and others had taken care to spread democratic ideas, an expedient was discovered in the establishment of a kind of constitutional monarchy, with the name of a republic, in which the hereditary monarch was supplied by an elected president; the upper house, by the senate; and the lower house, by the house of representatives. The whole was *mut. mut.*, an improved copy of constitutional monarchy, while its chief evils, separate executive power, the representative system, and its embodyment in two chambers, were retained.

—————o—————

THE PRESIDENCY AS A SEPARATE EXECUTIVE POWER.

There are but two systems of government founded upon logically consistent principles, — absolute monarchy, and absolute democracy.

Every form of government suspended mid way between these two opposites is an untenable compromise, and must sooner or later fall back into one, or, moving forward, be changed into the other.

True, absolute monarchy recognizes no rights of the ruled, and unites all powers, the law making, the executive, and the judiciary also, in the person of the monarch. Since the development of mankind however tends towards democracy, and absolute monarchy can neither suppress this tendency for any length of time, nor offer anything in place of it, it has been compelled in the course of time to make more or less concessions to it; and as, on the other hand, democracy was not yet strong and developed enough to render absolute monarchy incapable of doing harm, by abolishing the whole monarchical system, it was content with those concessions which consisted in a 'division of power'. This was the origin of so-called 'constitutional monarchies'. Since the times of Montesquieu, Europe had held the belief that in them had been discovered the political philosopher's stone, while in truth they are nothing else but the deceitful compromises of two opponents who affirm that they are laboring for a common aim, while, according to their different interests, they must always combat each other till one of them succeeds in annihilating the other; and since in the 'division of powers' the really decisive one, the executive power, armed with the sword, and in possession of the public treasury, was left in the hands of monarchy, democracy, of course, will naturally always have the worst of it in that struggle, unless, which is barely the case, the chief tool of the ruling power, the army, throws up its allegiance to its superior.

In spite of this plain defectiveness and danger, necessarily existing in the very nature of constitutional monarchy, and the division of power, the same order of things was transferred to the republic. It was supposed that a great difference was being constituted if, under the name of president, a king was *elected* instead of being *inherited*, if his government was limited to a certain time instead of being suffered during his life, and if the body politic was called a republic instead of a monarchy. Only the name, however, had been changed: in the main, the old order of things was retained. It was acknowledged that all power proceeded from the people, but one had forgotten to make sure, also, of the power remaining with the people. True to the old 'constitutional' superstition of the necessity of a 'division of powers', France 'put the chief force, the executive power, having command of the sword and the public treasury, which she had just wrested from a perjured king, into the hands of a perjured president, and then felt astonished on discovering one fine day to find the new republic strangled, and upon its coffin the president turned into an emperor.

But why do we speak of the French? They only followed the example set them by the greatest republic in the world, the North American. We only spoke of them first because they first put into decisive practice the example set by North America. It will be the question now whether this country shall heed the warning others have given it at their expense.

At the time when the North American colonies renounced their allegiance to England, the republican spirit, as we have mentioned before, was but little developed within their borders. They threw off the monarchical yoke not because it was monarchical, but because it pressed heavily on them. Had some English prince resided in the colonies at the time, who had sustained them in their opposition against the oppression of the mother country, they would immediately have placed him at their head, and later proclaimed him for the hereditary ruler. In default of a candidate for hereditary monarchy, they founded an elective monarchy. They attempted to manage by a mixture of monarchical and democratic institutions, at whose head they placed a president. Had they at that time been blessed with a Tyler or a Pierce, a Buchanan or a Johnson, they would probably have thought of establishing the executive power in some other shape; but since a Washington was at their head, they did not suspect that with a president they only set up a king in a dress-coat, in whose pockets decrees of usurpation and *coups d'état* might be concealed just as well as in the pockets of a Louis Napoleon.

The constitution of the United States establishes that the president is to be the executor of the laws proceeding from congress. But, neither constitutional nor legal regulations have ever yet answered their purpose where they were not directly sustained by material power, but rather opposed by a power capable of maintaining itself more or less independently from them. If the executor holds more power than the law-giver, the master is dependent on the servant, and the servant always tempted to make himself the master. In the very nature of things, it is only a matter of course that an executive power endowed with equal rights, and compelled to exist by the side of the law-making, will submit to the latter only with reluctance; that, supplied with all power to act, and at all times called on to act, it should feel superior to that political power which is only called on at certain times to deliberate and conclude; that, being the object of universal attention, the center of all political action, the organ of all national manifestations, and the source of all marks of power, it should ascribe to itself a higher importance, and more authority, than to an assembly, which, although it is intended to represent the people, has yet no head whose action is of any importance, and no means of direct manifestation; that, finally, in the full sense of its power and importance, it must be easily tempted to abuse that power by opposition to the powerless legislative branch, in order to carry out its own will, or perform acts of usurpation.

It is a vain undertaking to attempt to effectually prevent such danger by particular legal restrictions. If such restrictions go so far as to make the executive branch completely powerless to do harm, fetter it, so to speak, hand and foot; they, also, make it powerless to perform its office, render it, therefore, not only perfectly superfluous but even harmful through this powerlessness; does it, however, retain in its own hands the means of performing its office,—among which may be chiefly numbered the command of the army and navy, the management of the public treasury, the power to appoint and remove officials, to have the republic represented abroad, etc.—it thereby again possesses the means of manifesting its own will, and becoming dangerous to the republic. A. Johnson furnished the practical proof of the uselessness of the experiment to deprive a dangerous executive power of the ability of doing harm, by restricting laws on particular occasions. This danger, however, rises to its greatest hight if at extraordinary times, particularly in case of a war, all the powers of the country are placed at the disposal of the executive, when his judgment becomes the only leading, his will the only conclusive, one,—the fate of the whole people, in short, is put into his hands, and the whole republic learns to submit to the decision, obey the command, at the sign of a single man.

Before we speak of the warning experience has already given us on this hand, it is necessary to first glance at the privileged position assigned by the constitution itself to the executive power.

Already at his election it becomes apparent that the president occupies an exceptional position by his being elected not by the people direct, but by electors not bound to the will of the people.

After his election, he holds command not only of the army and navy, but also of all the militia in the country, in case it is called out. He has not the right to declare war, but if he desires it, he can easily bring it on with any foreign power through his secretary of State, or, as Mr. Buchanan showed us, encourage and passively prepare for it in the country.

By the royal right of pardon, his favor is placed above law and justice. Dispensation from punishment should proceed only from the same power that dictated the penalty, that is from the law-giver, the people.

In concluding treaties with foreign powers, he is dependent on the consent of the senate ; but, as Mr. Seward showed us, it is not difficult for him to force treaties secretly prepared upon the senate as well as the house of representatives in such a manner that they can not be rejected any more without compromising the government. General Grant, too, gave proof by his St. Domingo business what embarrassments and dangers may arise to the country from the right of the uncontrollable executive power to take the initiative step in foreign affairs.

He nominates the judges of the supreme court. He then, who is the first to have the temptation offered the power given him to violate the constitution, may make his creatures members of that court, whose office it is to decide upon violations of the constitution. Nay, more, he nominates in the judge of the supreme court the president of that tribunal which, in case of impeachment, is to judge himself! A right of this kind, where the possible criminal nominates his own judges in advance, is an anomaly that borders on a monstrosity.

He is to execute the laws of congress : he himself, however, is endowed with the power to make them laws first. Without his signature, the laws of congress are only propositions ; and if he refuses his signature, two-thirds of a legislative body of several hundred members are required to vote down the veto of a single man. Through these, altogether anti-democratic regulations, the constitution itself attributes to him not only greater importance and power than to the representatives of the people, but also, from the very outset brings about a conflict between them and him by first making a legislator of the executive, and then putting him into the position of being obliged to execute laws he first rejected by his veto.

An other ascendancy over congress is given to him by the power (borrowed from constitutional kings) of not only convening the representatives of the people but also adjourning them for any length of time (in case the two houses can not agree upon the term of adjournment).

All these exorbitant privileges of the president, all derived from the ' constitutional monarchies' of Europe, form, as almost insurmountable obstacles practically, the most glaring contrast to the provision according to which congress may call him to account, and summon him before its bar. The conception of accountableness presupposes decided *subordination*, the dependence of him who is called to account upon the one who is to call him to account. After all that we have shown, however, it appears that congress is more dependent on the president than the president on congress. The president has the means of power, congress only words; he may act, congress can only talk; he sends the legislative body to the capitol, and, if it so happens, home again: the legislative body must go to him 'at the other end of the avenue'. He has a thousand opportunities of showing or refusing some favor to the legislators; the legislators may at the most, in rare cases, refuse one of his creatures an appointment. Not only in the interest of their *protégés* but in their own interests they are thrown upon his favor, and many of them expect some office from him when their congressional term has expired. Under such circumstances, his accountableness before congress will not rob even the worst president of his night's rest, particularly since he is still further protected by the constitution through the provision that the representatives of the *people* have only the right to impeach him; and that two-thirds of the representatives of the *States* are required to convict him.

Now, if anything else were yet needed to encourage the president in any overbearing sense of the fulness of his power, and the most extended use he can possibly make of it, it is the hazardous arrangement which, according to the constitution, leaves him for nine months in the year, during the adjournment of congress, alone without any control at the head of the government. He may do or leave undone whatever he pleases during this long period of time. Congress, unless particular provisions to that effect have been made, has no right as well as no opportunity to oppose him,—in short, the country during nine months in the year is resistlessly at the mercy of the autocrat of the 'white house'. The Mexican constitution attempted to remedy this evil by establishing a permanent congressional deputation, whose office it is to watch over the executive during adjournment, and who also has the power of convening congress; but even this expedient, which may serve in ordinary times, can not on extraordinary occasions do away with the dangers necessarily arising from an executive power which is separate from the legislative.

If these dangers were ever brought close to the American people, it was during and after the war of the rebellion. If we imagine the case that in the year 1860, or even so late as 1864, an A. Johnson had succeeded in making himself president by the same deceptions that made him vice-president, we shall not doubt for a moment that today the North American republic would no longer exist,—that slavery would rule with an iron rod over its whole territory. What though would have been the essential cause of this calamity? Not the baseness of this A. Johnson, but the position in which he would have been placed, a position where the whole power of the republic would have been entrusted to the hands of one single, uncontrollable man. Fortunately, A. Johnson came into possession of power only after the war was at an end. A. Lincoln did not make use of his position for the subjugation of the republic through the slave-holders, but he, too, showed the people plainly enough in what manner he might have made use of it. The preponderance of the executive power which appeared already in so suspicious a manner under Pierce, and rose to a *regime* of unscrupulous brutality under Buchanan, under Lincoln, favored by the concentration of the immense forces of war, assumed almost the shape of an absolute, unlimited power. Not only friends of the rebels, but also many sincere friends of the republic, already at that time dubiously shook their heads over the possibility of a *coup d'état.* But if already a former rail-splitter, a flat-boatman, who was set up as a model of simplicity, and who enjoyed the full confidence of his party, could, when in the presidential chair, give rise to the idea of a *coup d'état,* this may well be to us the most serious inducement to examine closely the dangerousness of a position which gives to a single man command over a million of soldiers. Can, aye, must it not encourage a treasonable occupant to some outrage against the republic? Who would have the power to save the republic, if in some new war some fortunate general, having the army on his side, occupied the 'white house', and undertook to give a king to the people, dazzled by the glories of war, change 'His Excellency' into 'His Majesty'? Did not, even after the war of the rebellion was ended, when by the disbanding of the army the power of the president was reduced to a minimum, Lincoln's successor throw the country repeatedly into disgust and agitation by the excited expectation of a *coup d'état?* Did not his secretary of State, with autocratic overbearing, put to the people the alternative of 'president or king'? and who can assert that the expectations of a *coup d'état* would have been disappointed if the courage of the usurper had been equal to his desire, or if congress, by an impeachment, had put to the test the threat contained in his last message?

The sole weapon offered by the constitution against the abuse of the executive power, which already now yields nothing to any king on the face of the earth, in power and influence, is impeachment. But this sole weapon not only proved itself unserviceable at the very first attempt to put it in use, but was even received by him against whom it was turned with contempt and menaces. This attempt justified the worst fears in regard to the powerlessness of the legislative body over the executive; it showed us how far a president of this republic may carry his insolence, his want of principles, his arbitrariness, his lawlessness, his usurpations, without being called to account for it; it made manifest how much harm, how much ill treatment, how much contempt a republican people is obliged to suffer from a so-called public servant without being able to employ any lawful means to remedy the evil; it caused it to appear that in practice the president is as 'inviolable' as a constitutional king, while he has not, like the latter, a responsible ministry about him; it not only justified A. Johnson in repeating all the sins he had committed before, but encouraged him to even overstep yet the bounds within which he had so far kept; and finally it furnished a precedent to every one of his successors, which from the very outset must deprive him of all scruples as to any assumption of power that might go too far. If the deeds of A. Johnson did not bring about his removal from the 'white house', we can only think of such acts of violence yet, for sufficient causes for the deposition of a president, as would make him at the same time the all-powerful master of his judges. The French national assembly, too, at length condemned L. Napoleon for high treason, but the condemned man sent his judges to prison. But, even if none of A. Johnson's successors should overstep the bounds wherein he may abuse the powers of his office with impunity, the bounds conceded to them by the vote on the impeachment, this alone would be sufficient to render all constitutional guaranties worthless, for it needs only two successive Johnsons to ruin the republic, even without a *coup d'état*, unless, by the abolition of the presidency, all Johnsons are made impossible.

The presidency is more than any other office an office of confidence. Its dangerousness can only be covered for the time being by the complete justification of the confidence placed at his election in the occupant. But the majority of the presidents we have had so far did not justify the confidence placed in them, which speaks more for the corrupting influence of the office than gives proof that the occupants are unworthy of confidence. This experience should teach us anyhow that in a democratic body politic, where 'eternal vigilance' (that is, eternal mistrust) 'is the price of freedom', personal confidence should never take the place of constitutional guaranties. The confidence of the people must always become injurious after a while if they grant more power than they retain themselves to put a stop to the abuse of this confidence. The best constitution is certainly the one which makes confidence in the holder of the public power as superfluous as possible, by rendering any abuse of it as difficult as possible.

It is impossible, as has been shown above, to attain this object, and at the same time retain the presidency. But, even were it possible, without taking from him the means of carrying out the duties of his office, to so control the powers of the president that he should no longer be able to rise above the laws, or feel tempted to undertake any act of violence, the office would yet be incompatible with the weal of the republic, because of the president's position as the very center of party struggles, and a source of corruption.

When the presidency was established, it was regarded as a means of executing the will of the people, and of projecting the common interests. In this spirit, the first occupants of the office carried on the administration. Gradually it came to be regarded more and more as a means of satisfying the ambition of the candidates, and procuring for the leaders of the party that secured the victory to them the advantages at the disposal of the president. In former times, the victor had the honor of promoting the interests of the people; at a later period, nobody was abashed at proclaiming and carrying out the shameful maxim of 'to the conqueror belong the spoils'. The 'father of the republic' changed into the fathers of the booty-hunters. Principles that formerly determined the formation of parties afterwards served as bait for the voters,— the chief motive of the leaders and wire-pullers was booty. The presidency became the aim of every ambitious politician; to attain his aim, he was not only obliged to accommodate his principles to circumstances, but also to engage himself to every associate who might possibly have furthered his interests, and when the aim was attained, he was compelled to appoint to the offices on whose administration depends the weal of the country not those who might serve the people best, but those who would serve him best. Thus the whole struggle for the highest office in the republic became a chase for booty, and a traffic where regard for the public weal was set aside for the sake of personal interests, and where intrigue and corruption served as the most effectual means ; and when the struggle was over, and the victor in possession, there instantly began preparations to have the whole repeated. The whole power, and the immense patronage at the disposal of the victor, were now employed as means to secure his position for the next term also, or at least to maintain his party in possession of the booty. Thus the chief activity of politicians, which should be devoted to the public weal, consists from year's end to year's end in the pursuit of, and the struggle for, personal advantages, whose inexhaustible store-house is the 'white house'. To the 'white house' everything is drawn, from the 'white house' everything proceeds, and even the capitol is occasionally changed from a hall for the discussion of the interests of the people into a head-quarters of the struggle for the 'white house'. The 'white house' is the high school of corruption, as it is the seat of treason. Whoever shares the opinion that a republic can only live through the virtue of its citizens must believe this virtue capable of superhuman firmness, if he does not object to having it put to the test by the institution of the presidency. How many hundred millions in money the presidency has already cost the American people is difficult to calculate ; how much though the masses and their politicians have lost by it in public morals and genuine republican spirit appears daily everywhere in the most frightful manner. The institution of the presidency exerts so pernicious an influence that it becomes even questionable whether the president does not do more mischief before his election than after his inauguration,—for every campaign is a school for all the lies, intrigues, and evil passions that ambitious politicians, hungry for booty, can possibly make use of ; and the whole people is obliged to pass through this school without perceiving what a corrupting influence it exerts on public morals.

If the constitution of the United States should in future serve other nations for a model, this will not at least be the case, we trust, in regard to the institution of the executive power. When in 1848 the Swiss republic altered its constitution, it retained it is true two defective institutions which it shares with this country, that is, the constitution of the States (cantons), and the two-chamber system; but it took good care not to adopt the American institution of the *presidency*. According to its new constitution, its executive power consists in a confederate council of seven members, which, like the confederate court, is elected for three years, by the confederate assembly, from all the eligible citizens of the country. The members of this council elect their own president every year. The same person can not be president two years in succession. The council has no veto, and no right to grant either amnesty or pardon, which power is reserved to the legislative body. In case public safety demands the enrollment of troops, the council is obliged to convene the confederate assembly so soon as the number of troops to be enrolled exceeds 2000 men, or the enrollment lasts over three weeks.

All these arrangements give proof of the recognition of the dangers attending an executive power when it holds too much authority, and is exercised by one person. They make the executive power directly dependent on the legislative, and a sort of ministry to the confederate assembly; and this, the subordination of the executive to the law-making power, or the union of the two, is the great point. To divide them, place them on a footing of equality, or permit them to oppose each other, is just as illogical as it is undemocratic. In a democratic commonwealth, all power proceeds from the people, and just as little as the people themselves divide may the power divide that proceeds from them, and acts as their agent. The people are politically a unit, as a single individual is such; and as no individual has his ideas and resolutions carried out by a power separate from and outside of himself, so little do the people require a separate executive authority for the resolutions and laws they cause their legislative organs to adopt and establish. As the legislative body is the organ of the people, so must the executive power be the tool of the legislative.

———o———

THE EX-PRESIDENT.

An American knows no higher aim than to grow rich, or become president. Many, though, would certainly check their ambition if they had a clear picture in time of the contrast presented by the quiet farewell from the 'white house' at the expiration of the term to the loud triumph with which the fortunate candidate took possession of it. A mistress once adored and then deserted offers no sadder image of bitter vicissitude than a president for four years worshiped like an idol, and then perhaps sent home with imprecations. Even the worst president might after his dismissal disarm hatred by pity. Let us fancy the sun, who today shines upon all, and is admired by all, endowed with consciousness, and then tomorrow extinguished, to see his place taken by some former planet, and we shall have the picture of a man who today is the head of all heads, in the possession of all power, the object of the attention of all creatures, and then must suddenly go his way as an ordinary mortal, silent and unnoticed, betake himself off almost like a dismissed servant, in the midst of the noise and the shouts that accompany his successor to the throne he has just left. In truth, there is something of cruelty in this change of presidents. A king in the purple is at least fortunate enough never to see his successor, as such: he remains the worshiped king until he becomes unconscious food for worms, and the 'love' of his subjects, as well as the 'loyalty' of his servants, accompanies him until he reaches that point where love and loyalty, and power and glory, become entirely indifferent to him. But one of these kings in a dress-coat is obliged to see all the splendors in which he played a chief part suddenly change while he is yet in the possession of full consciousness, and must disappear in a corner behind the scenes as one who has no longer any business there; after he has become quite accustomed to the luxurious table of rulership, and his whole system has become filled and satiated with the rare dishes of ambition, he now sees himself suddenly ordered away from the table, forced to content himself again with the old, ordinary, frugal food with which every good-for-nothing among the 'people' keeps body and soul together. The presidents that were form a particular, and certainly not enviable, class of people; haunted all through life by the wants and pretensions engendered by their former prominent position, without the means and the chance to gratify them, they are a kind of artificially-produced geniuses who, after the expiration of their term, belong to the 'unacknowledged', and then suffer to the end of their days from the withdrawal of the tribute of admiration due them, and formerly promptly paid. Even among the Romans there was but one Cincinnatus. Among all the great men that survive themselves, the kings in dress-coats are the most pitiable, because their living death overtakes them so suddenly, and the neglect that succeeds it shows them with such cutting clearness that all the demonstrations of honor to which they have accustomed themselves were meant only for their position, and the marks of favor proceeding from it not for themselves, and as a tribute of respect to their personal worth; and how sharply must the contrast to the former homage be felt by a genius who, like the illustrious Johnson, hears already before he takes leave the moral kicks preparing for him, that wait for his appearance outside the door. We can not really find much fault with him that, at the very last he yet made use of, we may say the hour before execution, would eat his fill in an extra treat, and take something with him on the way that would make his transit easier; and this the excellent Johnson did, with all his power, when he was on the eve of taking his departure from the 'white house'. He kept a quantity of bills that congress had tired itself over in solemn discussions in his pocket, so they were nothing any more but so much waste paper; he left his enemies a sermon in which a four years' crop of gall was deposited; on the other hand, he liberated his best friends and brothers in spirit, that is, all the criminals his pardon could reach, the last traitors, forgers, pirates, and assassins of Lincoln included, in order to set them upon the villainous company that had not elected him again; and thus he departed, so to speak, with his tongue put out, and turned towards congress and mankind and his successor with an infernal, or goblin-like, "Aha!" That is the revenge of an ex-president. First, the presidency furnishes its occupant with all the means of corruption and misuse of power to maintain himself in office, but if he has not succeeded in this, it furnishes him with the means of making even his departure, which the whole people had the greatest desire to see, as pernicious as possible. Of a president it may be said,—he is an evil before he exists, an evil when he comes, an evil when he is there, and even an evil when he goes again.

———o———

THE PRESIDENT AND PARTY ORGANIZATION.

'In republics parties are a necessity'. This phrase is everywhere repeated as an axiom, and Solon is here quoted or an authority. Solon's precept, however, to join some party in the State only means that the citizens of the State are to take an interest in its affairs, that they are to lend their cooperation in the decision of questions concerning the public weal, and are not to leave it to those holding power, or to the politicians by profession, or the demagogues, only. In countries where the unquestioning obedience of good subjects is the order of the day, for instance, in Herr Bismark's empire', the law of Solon would be considered a sort of high reason : there no party is allowed to exist save that of those who hold the power. In a republic, however, öbedience to it is the first condition required to maintain liberty, and secure the rule of the people. Not to join a party here means to inactively surrender up the power of the citizens, and, under certain circumstances, it may mean the betrayal of the republic.

The question is now, however, to understand Solon's precept correctly, and not through a deceptive, mistaken interpretation permit it to be employed for false purposes. The taking of sides is in general the duty of the citizen ; but it may be still a higher political duty to take sides *against* the parties. The taking of sides must not be so interpreted as though it were a duty to support one of the *existing* parties. In the question which of two opposite parties is to be supported, the citizen must proceed from the supposition that one of them represents, according to his conviction, right, the other wrong. If he holds them both to be in the wrong, however, it is not his duty to join either, but rather to contend against both. Now, the chief point is whether *standing* parties, as they exist in this country, are necessary at all ; whether they do not even exert a pernicious influence. How, then, if it should be proved that standing parties are to be combated and abolished just as well as standing armies?

In the question of taking sides in a democratic republic, we must originally start from the single, independent individual, and entirely ignore the existence of parties already formed. Let us imagine now a commonwealth of twenty millions of such individuals, none of whom are yet compromised or bound by participation in any organization. Let some public question arise in this commonwealth,—the proposal for some regulation in the State, the draft of a law, a proposition concerning the constitution. The question is thoroughly discussed in meetings as well as by the press. The result is that these twenty millions take sides individually, according to their convictions and their interests, for and against the question, *without an organized party*, and that the will of the people is manifested freely and honestly, without secondary considerations. The citizens give their vote for or against the *question* under consideration, but not for or against the *party* that represents or combats it. Let us now imagine a second, entirely different question brought up after the one just disposed of, and the same manner of decision through independent individuals, perhaps millions who occupied the same position before now oppose each other as enemies. The result, however, is the same,—a taking of sides, without any binding-party, and the true expression of the will of the people on the question under consideration, without any regard to party advantage or party disadvantage. Through a proceeding of this kind, an independent taking of sides, without closed parties, we should approach also as near as possible to that which we call a representation of the minority. Had the controverted questions, however, been disposed of through party organizations already existing instead of through independent individuals, the decision would have resulted quite differently. Instead of the reasons for or against the matter to be decided, a looking to the advantage or disadvantage of the party would have turned the scale ; the single individuals would have permitted their votes to be dictated by the command of the party, instead of by the command of their own independent reason ; and not the spirit of truth and right, but *party spirit* would have been the leading one. Even if we assume that it would not be well possible to always maintain the independence of individuals, even when no organized parties are in existence, that in many cases it might be sacrificed to impure influences, and might not entirely exclude corruption, it yet would certainly never be endangered in whole masses by the powers and means of an organized party, nor paralyzed by the habit of following where others lead. The cases where it should succumb would remain single ones, would be of private nature, and could not on every occasion be repeated in the same manner, while an organized, permanent party continually practices them.

The great defect of standing parties, a defect brought about by this origin, and their striving after the possession of power, lies in this, that their chief aim is *rulership*, permanent rulership. Although originally perhaps first called into being by the purpose of carrying out certain principles or measures, they were yet, as bodies politic have so far been organized, always obliged to direct their chief efforts towards the overthrow of existing powers, so as not only to take authority into their own hands, but also retain it by every possible means. They attempted, therefore, to perfect their organization as much as possible, strengthened the ties of principle by the ties of corruption, and by discipline and intimidation made it a duty to join their ranks, while originally their members had come to them of their own free will. In this manner they came to gradually forget the aim that had called them into being, and to regard the continuance of their rule as the chief aim, to which every other was subordinated. The chief aim of their rule, however, became — ' booty ' ; and when this purpose is gained, the result is wont to be that they continue adding to corruption and the abuse of power till the measure overflows, and then an other party takes their place to play the same game over again. Thus the masses called the people are being continually drawn hither and thither in two organizations, to both of which they are continually lending their support, without in fact having much to say in either.

To remedy this evil there is no other means but to sustain a free taking of sides, to liberate it from the ban of organized parties, and reduce it as much as possible to the independence of individuals. The means of gaining this purpose, however, is to change that organization of power which makes it possible for one particular party to hold the rulership and its possession the chief aim of the party. Here the rule of this or that party is decided by a single act, on which all efforts are concentrated,—the struggle for the executive power, the presidential election. The result of this one election makes so and so many millions of the 'people', calling themselves 'democrats' or 'republicans', or rather their leaders, masters of the republic for four years at least. Let them do as much mischief as they please, their rule for these four years is assured, and by means of this rule their party keeps together, only anxious to prolong it as much as possible, while that portion of the people not belonging to this party has no means of manifesting itself. Would this condition be possible if ruling politics were not based on a power established for so and so many years, but were continually under the living influence of the people themselves? Could one party, as such, secure to itself exclusive power, if this power were exercised through organs or agents, determined in their actions at all times by every portion of the people? In a word, could the present party organizations, a public nuisance, continue in existence if the presidency and the senate were abolished, and their place were taken by a permanent assembly of agents of the people, that may be influenced by their electors at all times, and replaced by others? With such an arrangement, there would be no fixed center of power, of authority, and of patronage from which a standing party might be directed, and kept together. Politics would originate from below, not from above ; they would not be the fixed business of a party, but would accommodate themselves each time to the will of the people ; they would not be dictated by one portion of the country to an other, but independently influenced by every electoral district ; and the taking of sides would change according to the questions each time under consideration, instead of being pointed out for all cases by a party programme. Now there are only 'democrats' or 'republicans' in congress. Let the present support and center of party organization be destroyed, and the national assembly taking the place of congress will consist only of independent members, bound to each other by no party tie, and dependent only on their constituents. In this, it is true, a majority will decide that in chief questions shall be united by like convictions ; but this majority is no fixed one, formed only for party interests, one that was organized from the very outset ; it may change just according to the questions brought up for discussion, and can only exist by conformity with its independent electoral circles, that have not united for the maintenance of rulership, or the division of booty, but chosen the representatives of their principles and interests, according to their individual convictions.

———0———

THE REPRESENTATIVE SYSTEM.

Still more dependent than congress from the president, who ought to be its executing servant, is the so-called master of both, the people, from congress, that ought to represent it. The right of representation originated in Europe through a compromise of monarchy with democracy : in America it amounts actually to an *abolition* of democracy. Here representation does not mean the making good of the claims of the people through their attorneys opposite a power above and outside of the people, generally designated as the 'crown'; no, here it means the surrendering up of all rights of the people, all the intelligence of the people, and all the power of the people into the hands of the authorized agents, who, by means of their mandate, monopolize the whole business of the management, and the administration of the State. Here the representatives are, so to speak, the guardians through whose election the people make minors of themselves, and put themselves under guardianship. The election of a represenative, which the people regards as an act of the manifestation of its will, is only an act of resignation. After the election, no people exists any more; for a certain period of time it is entirely done away with, defenceless against and without a will towards its own representative. May it manifest to him its displeasure through the press, or in meetings, or by any other means,—practically, it has given up its sovereignty to him, and it depends on the representative only, whether he is inclined to pay any attention to the protest of his constituents or not. What he who is elected concludes, not what they who elect desire, is law. He commands, they must obey; and whoever has ceded his right must not expect to have as much regard paid him as one still in the full possession of it.

Strange to say, some cases have occurred where representing sovereigns were requested by the represented ones to resign their positions, because of bad conduct. (We call to mind, for instance, Messrs. Doolittle and Yates.) What was the result? The gentlemen so requested each time refused to obey; and they were right. They might have answered, —"You sovereign at home have resigned by my election; how do you arrive at the logic of believing you have the right to request me to resign? I am you, and you are nothing so long as I am. So long as I exist as your representative, you do not exist; and whoever does not exist, has no rights. I refuse your request as an absurd piece of arrogance. Possess yourself in patience till, after the expiration of my term, you receive back existence, and with it the right of 'abdicating' again in favor of an other sovereign." If congress, in company with the president, concluded to empty the pockets of the sovereign people to the last cent, for the benefit of its representatives, the sovereign people, unless they were willing to overthrow their much-praised constitution, would have no means of resistance; they would be obliged according to the constitution to lay down their last cent on the altar of the representative system until that period had arrived when they might choose new guardians for themselves. This would be a 'legally' irrefutable result of the representative system.

Some time ago the London *Spectator* observed that the people of the United States had outgrown their constitution. It would be more appropriate to say they were grown into their constitution. This may anyhow be said of any people who through their constitutions established powers that are obstacles to the continual exercise and direct manifestation of their will. Constitutions of such a character are all more or less straight-jackets, and the most absurd straight-jackets are the 'representative' ones. To comprehend the whole absurdity of the conception of 'representation', we must join it to the conception of the 'sovereign people'. The people, it is said, is everything,—it is the State, and the aim of the State; it is the power, and the sovereign; and this everything, this State, this sovereign, is (consider the whole contradiction of the phrase) represented; and towards whom? Towards itself! Represented not only in the sense that agents act in its name, no, the agents *take the place* of the sovereign who empowers them, they assume his position, they become sovereign themselves for a certain time, while the sovereign they 'represent' retains neither a will nor rights, neither authority nor the power to take the initiative, —in short, does not legally exist at all any more. The people elects its 'representatives' not to give them business to execute, but to itself disappear for a time, for the benefit of these representatives. After the election, the people is nothing any more : its servants are everything. The people is only the master in order to make its servants its masters ; it only possesses rights to yield them up to those whom it should regard only as tools in the exercise of these rights.

The necessary consequence of this preposterous relation is an inconsiderateness towards, and a contempt of, the people, in the capitol as in the 'white house', and among the governors and legislatures of the single States, which no longer shrinks from any arbitrary act, nor any corruption. Do we perceive in a single one of these gentlemen in congress, or in the legislatures, that they regard themselves as tools to carry out the will of others, as agents for the dispatch of the business of others? Do they show the least regard for the many-headed sovereign when they squander his money, waste time, neglect business, raise their salary and their mileage, supply themselves with stationery articles, retain their shameful franking privilege, squander the public lands, apply themselves to corruption with the 'representative' at the other end of the avenue, or with the lobby, adjourn for weeks over the 'holy days', devote all their energies to presidential intrigues instead of to the interests of the country? Could they act more sovereignly and more regardlessly if the 'sovereign' they 'represent' had entirely disappeared from the earth?

The disadvantage, however, which accrues to the people from the representative system consists not only in this that it makes their representatives careless of their desires and interests, but in something that proves much worse in the course of time, the fact that it accustoms the people to the most patient, most apathetic endurence of all evils the rulers of their fortunes may prepare for them. Submitting to it 'according to the constitution', that after the election it practically does not exist any more as a sovereign power, the people, according to the constitution, suffers everything its chosen representatives do and leave undone, so that in fact its political activity, which should never slacken, is reduced to the act of election only, and it learns to seek in this mere act of election all its aid and comfort. Without this thoughtless habit, and this apathy, it would be quite inexplicable how accusations like those of Mr. Washburne, who represented his colleagues in general as the greatest swindlers, or those of Senator Sprague, who calls the congress composed of corrupt lawyers, and men of wealth the destruction of the republic, should remain without any consequences; it would be inexplicable how the people should continually suffer without serious opposition the perfectly gigantic corruptions whose mediator congress is, and particularly the unprincipled squandering of the public lands. Whoever read only the speech in which Mr. Julian of Indiana on the 21st of January, 1871, in the house of representatives reproached congress with the crimes committed by throwing away hundreds of millions of acres of the best land. belonging to the people, and to be made use of by the people, upon railroad companies, capitalists, and other speculators, he should certainly imagine the whole people would rebel against those who so outrageously and so shamelessly abuse its rights and its property. The people murmured a little here and there, and then was silent as usual: it knows that the theft committed against it is 'lawful', that it has itself elected the thieves, and then — it is *represented*!

And thus matters will remain so long as the people does not secure to itself a constitutional right to send home its law-making agents so soon as they act against its interest, and, moreover, reserves to itself the *approval or rejection of all the more important laws and conclusions* proceeding from these agents. Let us put only this one question,— would a squandering of land ever have taken place if the people had had a voice in the matter? Their 'platforms', those election-baits, the politicians very willingly let the people ratify, but to let it ratify their laws, their grants of land, their assessment of taxes, which acts practically answer the question after the execution of those most promising platforms, would never enter their minds.

———o———

THE TWO-CHAMBER SYSTEM.

Almost more contradictory yet than the combination of democracy with representation is the division of that representation into two chambers. One of these chambers represents that part of the people which constitutes the union, or the nation, and the other that part of the same people which constitutes the States of the union, or portions of the union, and in such a manner that the union-people may contend against and paralyze the States-people, and the States-people the union-people. It is just as though the people were afraid of itself, and were obliged to fetter its own limbs to be safe from its own will. But this contradiction is not the only one. The smallest State sends, in true democratic spirit, just as many representatives to the senate as the largest, and the again truly democratic consequence of this is that the people occasionally upsets its own majority when the States having the smallest population vote down those having the largest. Ten States, each with 100,000 inhabitants, may entirely paralyze nine States, each with 10,000,000, and annul all the resolutions they may have made in the so-called popular house.

It may also occur that the two votes which a State, as such, gives in the senate annul the thirty and more votes which the inhabitants of the same State give in the house of representatives. If this is democracy, it ought to be defined somewhat after this fashion,—Democracy consists in the artifice of procuring for the smallest possible minority the government over the largest possible majority. To such an absurdity we are quite logically brought however by that thoughtlessness which attempts to escape the specter of a united State, that is, of a united people, by shutting up that people in separate cages, and then secures to those cages a particular representation towards their assembled inhabitants.

————0————

THE SUPREME COURT.

Besides the fiction which concedes to the States, as such, particular rights, particular wisdom, and therefore, also, a particular representation, to guard themselves from themselves, that is, the very people that constitute it, we must not forget that fiction which intended establishing in the supreme court an independent protection for the people against their own justice. The unremovable board of the supreme court stands for a sovereign representation, as a power for pronouncing sentence, as congress stands a power for making laws ; and the court is even placed above congress as a decisive expounder of the laws. If, however, all sovereignty and power rests with the people, the people must reserve to themselves the right to have a last word to say in matters concerning the courts as well as in matters of legislation. It is true that the position of the judges should be as independent as possible, so that they may not be exposed to ordinary influences ; but this independence can not be an unqualified one towards the whole people without destroying the conception of democracy, and occasionally making the judges masters of the State. Moreover, the supreme court of the United States suffers under the strange defect of its members being creatures of the executive power, which lends a peculiar coloring to its pretended independence, and under certain circumstances might disturb the celebrated equilibrium of the three 'coordinate powers' in a serious manner.

As it was attempted' to render slavery and the presidency harmless by all kinds of patching, and laws made for the occasion, and no one perceived that this purpose could only be gained by their abolition, so efforts were made to exorcise the dangers connected with the power of the supreme court by occasional changes, without examining into the nature of its whole position. Already Jefferson considered this position of uncontrollable judges nominated for life venturous in the highest degree, and proposed to nominate them for five or six years only, and empower the president and the senate to remove them. But this proposition does not go to the bottom of the evil either. The chief objectionableness to the supreme court, as that to the president and to congress, consists in its undemocratic position, inaccessible to the people, and in this position it is moreover protected by the old prejudice, which makes, so to speak, superior beings of the judges, is wont to surround them with a mysterious glory, a sort of worldly holiness ; and when, corresponding to this, these superior beings appear in the imposing uniform, in black robes and white ermine, no one thinks of remembering any more that such venerable figures rise from the people, and ought to be dependent on the people,—the people, whose pockets, under certain circumstances, might be emptied, and whose heads cut off, at their command. A court-room appears to people like a church, where even Americans take off their hats ; and even if the people is here liberated from that petty tyranny of monarchs which sees a particular crime in the 'offence against an official', it yet permits a 'contempt of court' to be looked on as a crime, in such a manner that a judge has a right of imprisoning the sovereign citizen according to his pleasure, because he does not treat him as though he were a superior being. This whole worship of the court is simply based on tradition, superstition, thoughtlessness, and humbug. It is true that it is necessary that particular persons, possessing the requisite knowledge, and whose character inspires confidence, should act as judges ; but these judges should have no privileges more than other servants of the people ; and the people should always secure to itself the right and the means to judge its judges, as all its other servants ; and it is certainly the destruction of all democracy that certain persons, placed like inviolable saints above the level of the people, are to dictate as the highest authority to the people what is right or wrong, what lawful or unlawful. From the people must proceed the legislative, from the people the executive, from the people the judiciary power ; and it must be accessible to the people through their chosen representatives. These representatives are first of all the legislators ; and as the executive, so should the judiciary power be subordinate to the legislative. Why should a judiciary commission of congress not be able to pronounce on the justice of some decision, or the constitutionality of some law, just as well as the wise heads of the supreme court? Are the judges, however, not to be nominated by the law-making agents of the people, then ought they to be elected by the people itself, and the people reserve to itself their removal, in the same manner as the change of those agents.

COORDINATE POWERS.

It will not be superfluous to examine also the much-praised coordination of powers, looked upon as the most profound statesmanship, under a magnifying-glass.

The constitution of the United States fixes the purpose and the authority of the three powers that are to act as the political organs of the people, without by special regulations defining their relation to each other. It nowhere speaks of 'coordinate powers'; but it was intended to practically establish that which is generally designated by that term, and this was established. Each of the three powers — the legislative, the executive, and the judiciary — should, existing beside the two others, perform the ·duties of the sphere assigned it in such a manner that the activities of all should work together for one harmonious whole, and it was supposed that this would be the realization of the constitutional ideal.

Upon a closer examination, we discover that these institutions are based upon a great mistake, and that a contradiction was with them admitted into the State mechanism, which might remain silent for a while, but could not be suppressed for any length of time. The three powers may be represented as three horses before the car of State. Guided by a coachman, they may carry their load evenly and harmoniously; without a coach-man, they would infallibly collide, particularly if it were intended that they should not only draw together, but also check or clog each other. If the organs called State powers could act quite independently of each other, there would be a possibility for each to fulfil its purpose without encroaching on the rights of the other, or having its own rights encroached on, —*provided* there should exist again some higher power to guide them all towards one common aim. But they are to be not only dependent on each other, by mutually supplying and completing each other's activity, but they are also to watch over each other, and in this complicated activity show and exercise the united highest power and authority, that is, that of the people, in a representative manner; and this they are to do, endowed with equal rights, placed in equal positions, 'coordinated'. Let us now see how this relation of coordination appears in practice.

Congress makes the laws. As traditional political views left no room for the idea that he who makes the laws could and should execute them too, but considered a particular executive power necessary, a president was instituted. To make this president expressly and unconditionally a servant of congress, as logically his executive destination would have required, was considered somewhat venturous. As the senate was to serve as a brake on the house of representatives, so the president was to serve for a brake on both. He was therefore not subordinated to congress, but placed opposite to it, and authorized to annul its laws if possible by his veto; and where he would not or could not do this, execute them with the power put at his disposal alone. Now is congress coordinate with the president, and the president with congress? Congress, as a legislator and a judge, is the superior of the president, but through his veto it is his subordinate again, and without his power it is nothing at all. The president as an executor is the servant of congress; but, armed with the veto, the military forces, the public treasury, the power to appoint all officials, and have the republic represented abroad, he is its master: and how is the relation of both to the supreme court? Congress is to decide on the arrangement of the supreme court, and also be a judge of its judges; at the same time, however, these same judges are the authority for the laws of congress; and the president is actually made the appointer of these judges, whose presiding officer, in case of impeachment, is to be *his*, the president's, judge.

May this be called coordinate? Coordinate only in contradictions! All three powers are both the superiors of and subordinate to each other at the same time. But what they are not, and can not be, is of equal rank,—'coordinate'. They *must* occasionally jar therefore, and the events of the last years have given proof how much trouble it costs to silence and hush up their conflict by shifts and expedients, and laws made for the occasion. But this conflict will arise again, and not be set at rest before true democracy makes an end of it,—a democracy which knows and suffers to exist no other power but that directly established, dependent upon, and directed by, the people.

Let politicians meanwhile remember that the term 'coordinate powers' is not only an empty phrase but an actual lie, —in short, that no really coordinate powers exist, or can exist, in the State.

THE COMPROMISE OF FREEDOM WITH SLAVERY.

The third compromise we are to expose is that of freedom with slavery. This, however, has within the last ten years been exposed already in the red light of the torch of war in such a manner that to enter upon the subject in detail would appear as a waste of words. We shall say but one word here upon a clause in the constitution, which we have that compromise to thank for. It is characteristic of the young days of the republic from the outset, that it was more liberal in its views when it ran away from its master than when it became its own master. In its declaration of *independence* it established the equality of the rights of all men; in its declaration of *rights*, however, the constitution, it immediately introduced inequality. Yet this was not done without some shamefacedness. To preserve at least the appearance that, in spite of the connivance at slavery, that demand of the declaration of independence, according to which 'the governed must be represented in the government', was being respected, the slaves, three-fifths of them, were indirectly represented too, of course not in their own interest, but in that of their masters. This might be called a compromise between man and beast. As a man, a whole man, the slave was not to be acknowledged, or he would have had to be represented not by three- but by five-fifths, and by his equals; nor was he to be regarded as a beast, or either all representation must have been denied him, or other working animals, as horses and oxen, must have been admitted to congress for representation also. What, then, was done? The slave was made a *beast-man*, and the grace shown him to acknowledge him three parts man and two parts beast. In all cases the beast-man, who was not and could not be a citizen, was admitted to representation in the constitution of the United States. The question we now have to ask is this,—have *women*, who are everywhere acknowledged five-fifths of human beings, and also citizens, less right to representation than the former beast-men? That they are already represented by the men, as is often asserted, *of that the constitution says not a word*, possibly because the fifth question puzzled its authors. Consequently they are, according to the constitution, placed even below the former slaves, that is, *not represented at all*, neither directly nor indirectly, and yet they belong to the 'governed',—aye, they are nothing else but governed, the governed *par excellence*. If this shameful conclusion, that the glorious republic places women legally even below the former slave, or beast-man, is not to be drawn, there is but one way to save its honor, that is, the acknowledgment that their quality as citizens of the republic comprehends the complete equality of their rights.

lic. It guaranties to the single States a 'republican form of government', without, however, explaining by a word what is to be understood by this; it also secures to the citizens of the whole country the right of *habeas corpus*, and of trial by jury, protection against arbitrary searches, or seizures of their houses or property, etc.; but the chief liberties, that first lend value and stability to all the others, it indirectly abandons to the single States. Entire exclusion from the right of voting, that was formerly permitted in consideration of the slave-holders, is now, when there are no more slave-holders, save the male sex, abolished, it is true, save in regard to women; but the laying down of the conditions as to the exercise of this right of voting in the single States is still left to those States themselves. In the same manner the constitution surrenders to them religious liberty, the freedom of the press. etc. It permits the States to do everything it does not expressly prohibit, or reserve to itself. It prohibits. for instance, the issue of paper money, the laying of any duty of tonnage, and so forth; but it does not forbid them to 'legally' silence an abolition speaker, to 'legally' imprison an atheistical writer, to 'legally' exclude an unbeliever from office. Neither does it prohibit laws concerning Sunday, the oath upon the bible, and other religious restrictions and regulations, by which the personal rights and liberties of persons of opposite convictions are violated. All this only congress is expressly forbidden to do, by the regulation according to which no law is to be made abridging the freedom of speech, or of the press, the free exercise of religion, or the right of the people to peaceably assemble, and no religious test required as a qualification to any public office. These guaranties for the union on the whole are worthless however, or illusory, if the single cantons of the union may overthrow them at pleasure. That they may do so, and that in a most barbarous manner, is shown by the draconic laws often enough employed in the former slave and Puritan States, for whose sake the constitution established no *general* guaranty for the chief liberties of a democratic commonwealth.*

With these remarks we may close the general review of the constitution of this country. It has shown us that this celebrated constitution is in the main points entirely undemocratic, that it must render impossible a true democracy, a general, effective, and sure manifestation of the will of the people; and the history of the present as well as the past shows by a thousand facts that this theoretical conclusion finds complete confirmation in practical reality. The real people is in America, as well as in Europe, little more than a voting and paying machine; and, with the best of intentions, it will never bring about a change so long as it considers its constitution an ideal.

———o———

SKETCH OF A NEW CONSTITUTION.

In conclusion there yet remains the task of sketching in brief the changes to which this constitution should be subjected. They are as follows.

The former union of republics must be declared *one, indivisible* republic, and the former States, more practically divided, made provinces, that, after the abolition of their expensive legislatures, have their special affairs settled by circuit deputies.

The presidency and the senate must be abolished; the house of representatives, however, changed into an assembly

---

* How few guaranties are offered by the constitution against the annihilation of the most important rights by the single State was shown but quite recently by a 'law' of the New York legislature, which, except for the governor's veto, would have, in view of the corruption of the courts, completely fettered the freedom of speech and of the press.

of agents or deputies of the people, in permanent session, who may be instructed by their constituents, or replaced by others, at any time. The executive power, as well as the legislative, rests with the house of the deputies of the people, that has its laws executed, and the general business of administration attended to, by an executive and administrative commission chosen from among its own members, or from among the people, and to be controllable and removable by the house of deputies.

All more important laws are to be submitted to the people to have a particular vote taken on them, and only become valid by their direct approval.

If business permits, the house of deputies may adjourn for a certain time, maintaining its permanence, however, by a deputation which, during the time of adjournment, is to watch over the executive commission, prepare necessary questions for the next session, and in urgent cases convene the assembly in an extra session.

The fundamental rights that are to be laid down, conclusively and in detail, must not be contradicted either by the general laws of the republic, nor by special regulations in the provinces.

The provinces, circuits, and municipalities are to have the disposal, according to generally accepted rules, of all local interests, and all affairs not concerning the general public weal; but in doubtful cases, the house of deputies is to have the decision in the matter.

The courts are to be made as independent as possible, but remain subject to the control of the people; and the house of deputies shall be the last court of appeal, above the supreme court.

In the selection of deputies, the electors are not to be limited to persons from their own circuit, but may make their choice within the boundaries of the whole republic, — an arrangement by which the employment of the best and most independent powers of the country, and the manifestation of the desires of all shades of party, are made sure of.

These would be the chief points in a constitution in which the democratic principle, logically carried out, would be embodied, and which might fulfil all the conditions, drawn up above, necessary to a real government of the people.

It is true that even the best of constitutions is not alone able to attain that purpose. The last question always remains, what use the people would put it to. If the mass of the people be indolent, unprincipled politicians will make use of even the best of constitutions for the disadvantage of the people; if the people be bigoted and ignorant, its incapacity of judging will expose it to being misled and abused; if it be financially dependent on a wealthy minority, the complete assertion of its rights will be doubly difficult. Political reformation, then, can not be a radical cure for all evils without the so-called social reforms that are to make education and cultivation, and economical or financial independence, as general as possible. But political reformation is the indispensable condition for those other reforms: only through it will the needful freedom and opportunity be gained for the manifestation of all social wants and interests; and while it works thus, while a truly democratic constitution introduces the whole people into the political arena, and makes the means by which it may manifest its will as easy of access as possible, it at the same time opens to it the only school where it may attain to the full qualification for independent citizenship. It is a dogma established, with mathematical incontestableness, that the improvement of social conditions goes on in closest proportion to the degree of freedom established, and the participation of the people in political action. Only by way of democracy can, the 'social problem' ever be solved: the first of all 'social', as well of political questions, all over the world is, therefore, true democracy.

www.ingramcontent.com/pod-product-compliance
Lightning Source LLC
Chambersburg PA
CBHW022025080426
42733CB00007B/735